A SPORTING PRODIGY

The Sporting Misadventures of an 80-something Potteries Lad

Brian Mate

First published 2018
Cox Bank Publishing Limited
Brook House, Brook Lane
Coxbank, Audlem, CW3 0EU

web: www.coxbankpublishing.com

Copyright © Brian Mate 2018, 2019

All rights reserved. No part of this publication may be reproduced, stored in a retrieval system, or transmitted, in any form or by any means, without the prior permission of the Publisher.

ISBN 978-0-9956672-9-7

Front cover artwork and illustrations by Scartoons
Cover design by Marketing Bi Design, Stoke-on-Trent

Printed and bound by Panda Press, Stone, Staffordshire

CONTENTS

1. The Sporting Misadventures of an 80-something Potteries Lad — 8
2. Football — 9
3. Rowing — 13
4. Tennis — 16
5. Subbuteo — 18
6. Roller Skating — 20
7. Cricket — 24
8. Athletics — 27
9. Rugby and Hockey — 28
10. Table Tennis — 30
11. Snooker — 32
12. Cycling — 34
13. Golf - Part 1 — 37
14. Squash — 39
15. Golf - Part 2 — 40
16. A Football Manager — 44

17. Golf - Part 3	49
18. Walking	52
19. Gym	54
20. Stoke City and Port Vale	56
21. Programme Sellers	58
22. Autograph Hunters	60
23. Port Vale	64
24. Stoke City	71
25. Arsenal	75
26. The League Cup Final 1972	77
27. Boxing	83
28. Water Polo	86
29. Speedway	88
30. Wrestling	89
31. Kenny	92
Also from Cox Bank Publishing…	94

1. THE SPORTING MISADVENTURES OF AN 80-SOMETHING POTTERIES LAD

I planned the epitaph on my gravestone many years ago. It will read

'Loads of enthusiasm, not much talent'.

I think that the pattern of my life started when I was at infant school, where I looked forward to the music lesson with the drums, tambourine, triangle and maracas. Unfortunately, I never made it past the triangle.

My name is Brian Mate. I lived with my parents at their fruit and vegetable shop in Weston Road, Meir. I went to Meir Infants and Primary school before passing the eleven plus exam to Longton High School. With no ambition (perhaps wrongly) to go to university or teacher training college, I spent the next 50 years in the construction industry as a surveyor, estimator, building firm owner, project manager on a number of large local contracts and, in the last ten years of my working life as a building consultant when I was known as 'the red ash man', carrying out over eleven thousand sulphate floor tests on domestic properties throughout North Staffordshire and beyond. I married my wife Dot in 1960 and we have two children and three grandchildren. Always keen on sport, as a 'sportsman' my first love was always…

2. FOOTBALL

My sporting career started at Meir Junior School when a wonderful young teacher Mr Hancock was in charge of the football team. We had a couple of practice games before he picked his final 12 - 11 players and a reserve in case of illness or injury. Now this was just after the end of the war when clothes were rationed. Our strip was blue with many of them torn and in very poor condition. Mr Hancock launched an appeal and he got enough clothes coupons to buy a complete new strip, red tops with white sleeves. It was not until years later that I realised that those tops were the same as the Arsenal strip. More about them later in the story.

In our first game of the season we were still in our torn blue tops but I did not care as I was picked to play at right half. To play the game the two teams met at the school from where we walked with our noggins on as we called our football boots, nearly a mile to the pitch in Box Lane with its sloping pitch, iron goalposts, no nets of course and almost devoid of grass except a few tufts in each corner. I must have played ok as I was picked for the next game still wearing my torn blue strip with another home game and a nearly one mile walk to the pitch. This time we were playing Woodhouse School from Longton with their 'star' player Spooner. He played at inside left so he was my direct opponent. I spent the whole game chasing shadows and I think that we lost the game 4-0.

The next game was the first in our new Arsenal strip but when Mr Hancock came to tell us on Friday afternoon who would be playing, I was relegated to reserve. I spent the rest of the season as the enthusiastic and reliable reserve and never got to wear that Arsenal shirt. I have to say that as events unfolded many years later I was glad that I never had to wear an Arsenal shirt.

Like many boys who loved playing football I played at some time in the day nearly every day of the week. Our stadium was the backs, the passage between the backs of the terraced houses. We thundered up and down the backs with the goal at each end. My friend Kenny and myself were the star players mainly because most of the other kids were either younger than us or were girls. The only interruption to our games was when either the ball burst or it was kicked into Mrs. Bentleys yard, as she kept it - usually until the next day.

In addition, I played every lunch time in another backs half way between the school and home, much to the constant annoyance of my mother as I often only had about 20 minutes to eat my lunch before returning to school. On Sunday morning I would go to chapel in Uttoxeter Road. Next to the chapel was a garage with a large garage door, the ideal location for yet another kickabout. Even on Sunday afternoon I would smuggle my football boots into my bicycle saddle bag to play all afternoon at the Box Lane pitch. Now, you would have thought that with all that enthusiasm for the beautiful game I would have been someone every football scout had noted in his little book but the reality was that I could not even get into the school team never mind the dream of playing at Wembley or even the Victoria ground the home of The Mighty Potters so, as winter passed into summer, my thoughts turned to…

3. ROWING

Now Kenny and I were good rowers and Saturday afternoon on Longton Park lake was a great opportunity to show off our skills. We waited patiently in the queue for a boat to come free giving the boatman our 6 pence for half an hour. The problem was that there were many other 6 pence for half an hour boats on the lake so if you got three strokes in without hitting another boat with the boatman shouting at us, you were lucky. After half an hour his voice would boom out "come in number 5" or whatever your boat number was. We were wise to this however and after 25 minutes you made sure that your boat was hidden out of his view by the island in the middle of the lake. You then got at least an extra five minutes as well as more earache from the boatman.

Another summer sport to enjoy was…

4. TENNIS

   To fill our school holiday afternoons Kenny and myself would ride our bikes to Stone Road Rec. or Longton Park. I had my Dad's tennis racket which in those days weighed a ton and had a wooden frame that you had to put the racket into and screwed tight to keep the frame from becoming distorted. We had about six tennis balls which we marked so that we knew they were ours, or at least we had when we started playing. I think that there were three courts at Longton Rec and four at Longton Park. If all the courts were full you had to wait until one came empty and, unless you were very lucky an official looking man with a flat peaked cap came to collect your money in exchange for his ticket recording how much time you had.

   As the weeks went by naturally our tennis improved to the point where we could hit three or four shots each before the ball hit the net or sailed off the court. Unfortunately, there were a number of problems. Firstly, we did not have Hawkeye technology so there were frequent arguments about who had won the point. The other major problem was that there were no ball boys or girls. With all the courts having no fence between them, we spent half the time chasing after our balls from the next court or they were doing the same to us. When television arrived and we saw Wimbledon with Rod Laver, Lew Hoad and Ken Rosewall, yet again we realised that they were playing a different tennis to the tennis we were playing so when autumn arrived it was the perfect time to head indoors to play…

5. SUBBUTEO

In the 1950s there was no internet or i-phone so the iconic and most popular football game for boys was Subbuteo with its 20 cardboard players with a weeble bottom and two goalkeepers with weeble bottoms and a wire sticking out of the back. The goals even had nets, something we were not used to when playing school football. I cannot remember the scores as we flicked our star players, but I must have scored a few great goals, even beating the Vale on occasions. The good thing was that we did not have a referee to surround and argue with or a VAR screen in the next room but it was a great way to spend every Sunday evening with my friends. Another winter sport that attracted my attention was…

6. ROLLER SKATING

  I first learned to roller skate like many other children at the outdoor rinks while on holiday at either Rhyl or Llandudno so when we came home with our new-found talent, it was off to the Ideal Skating Rink in Town Road, Hanley with my friend Kenny. We went on Stoniers bus to Hanley, walking up Town Road to the rink (where Barclays Bank is now) where we queued to get our roller skates hoping to get a pair that fitted over our shoes with all 4 wheels going in the same direction. We probably spent the first 20 minutes of the two-hour Saturday afternoon session sorting all that out before joining about 200 others, hopefully all going the same way around the rink. When the rink was not too full a great game was for about 20 of us to link hands with the boy or girl nearest the middle of the rink pulling the others round. The one in the middle was hardly moving whilst the one on the outside was probably doing 25 miles an hour. That was fine until someone's hands became detached sending the rest crashing into the barrier.

  After nearly two hours of non-stop roller skating it was off down the road to Dericott's for a newspaper full of fish and chips, occasionally then going down Piccadilly to the old Hanley Museum to gaze at the stuffed animals. The other shop that was a magnet was Woolworth's with those large wooden counters and acres of things to buy. As well as my sporting prowess, I was a stamp collector something many boys did which now seems not to be cool. Anyway, one

Saturday I saw this stamp album that I really wanted. It was one and threepence (about 6p). When I checked what was in my pocket, I found a South African shilling, an Irish penny, an Australian penny and one English penny. I picked up the stamp album and offered the lady behind the counter my 'illegal' coins. Without looking carefully, she dropped the money in the till and I had got my stamp album, which I still have, for one penny. Good job Woolworths is no more otherwise they would be putting out a warrant for my arrest. Then it was back home on Stoniers bus probably with change out of two shillings (10p!!).

  When spring arrived, it was time to play…

7. CRICKET

To my knowledge my Dad never played cricket, but he took me as a young boy to local matches and to Test Matches at Old Trafford and Trent Bridge. He bought me a proper cricket bat and I was on my way to being the next Donald Bradman. Again, our Lord's cricket ground was the backs with a pile of clothes as the wicket. Again Kenny and myself were the star players as most of the others had butter fingers or were afraid that the ball would hit them. If you managed to hit the ball out of the backs that was a 4 but if you managed to hook the ball over the terraced house roofs and into the main road that was a 6. If you hit the ball into Mrs. Bentley's yard, that was the end of cricket for the day. Now, only Kenny and myself could hook the ball over the house roofs but that was to have disastrous consequences when I hooked the ball through Betty's fish shop back bedroom window. I think that I had to get the deposit back on a few pop bottles to pay for the replacement glass.

A man who was friends with my Dad, Mr Moore, played for Blythe Colours and was an excellent spin bowler. This was before the days of organised Kidsgrove league junior cricket but I would go in the evening to practice in the nets. The reward for all enthusiasm and dedication was not a place in a team but that of second team scorer. At least I got to travel with the team but unfortunately not in the white sweater, shirt and trousers.

The next season I moved to a bigger club, Longton, in pursuit of fame and fortune as a cricketer but although I would spend three nights a week in the nets I never got spotted as even a local club player.

 By this time I was 12 and at Longton High School, an all-boys school at that time. We were divided into 6 houses and competed against each other at athletics, cricket, rugby and hockey. Fame and adulation was just around the corner. I was selected for the house cricket team batting at number 10 of course, but at least it was one step up from the number 11 spot.

   We reached the final and needed 4 to win as I made my way on that long walk to the crease. I asked the umpire for middle and leg for no particular reason other than that almost everyone else did. I survived three or four balls before I swung at the ball - I can't say that it was a proper cricket stroke and I probably had my eyes shut at the time- but the ball hit the middle of the bat, sailed over the head of the nearest fielder and went over the boundary line for four runs. We had won the final of the house cricket competition and I was a hero. Even after that moment to savour I never made it higher than tenth in the batting order. The other summer sport at school was…

8. ATHLETICS

Now I had serious problems with athletics. Whilst I could run the rest of my efforts were not average school attainment never mind Olympic standard. I could not be relied on to throw a cricket ball from the boundary, or long stop where I usually found myself, to the wicket keeper so the javelin, discus and shot putt were non-starters. In the high jump it was a case of running head on at the bar before tripping over it if it was more than 3ft high and thankfully we did not have any hurdles to add to my embarrassment.

So that just left running. The problem there was that one of the boys in my class was the English Schools Champion at both the 100 and 220 yards so when we competed in the school sports he would finish the 100 yards about 20 yards ahead of me and about 40 yards in front of me in the longer race. Fortunately, he finished yards ahead of everyone else in the races so nobody seemed to notice me coming in in fifth or sixth place. He was a really talented sprinter and I am sure that that he would have gone on to be possible Olympian. Unfortunately, he damaged his knee ligaments playing Saturday morning rugby for the school so he was never able to test his potential against the rest of the world. For me, a quick dash up and down the backs with my friend Kenny was as good as it got. When the winter term started it was time to hone my skills at…

9. RUGBY and HOCKEY

I started playing rugby knowing that I was never going to be in the scrum as, at that time, you probably could not see me if I stood sideways. It was my position to play at the back but when I stepped aside at the sight of a big ugly youth from the scrum thundering towards me with an oval ball under his arm rather than make a brave tackle and risk breaking my spectacles it became pretty obvious that rugby was not for me. If we did not fancy rugby or if, like me, you had absolutely no appetite for violence you could move on to hockey which, in many ways, was more violent than rugby. Now I did enjoy playing hockey despite making very little impact on the game until someone rapped me with a hockey stick anywhere from the ankles upwards.

It seemed to me that it was time to seek excellence at something other than a team sport so at that point I started to play…

10. TABLE TENNIS

   Now I had recently joined the youth club at Meir School where, in addition to the usual team games, you could play table tennis. The problem was they only had one table for about 200 kids but fortunately only about 15 wanted to play. It seems strange in today's world that there were no girl players. It was obviously a boy's toy. The table was available from 7.00pm to 9.00pm on five evenings a week. The other problem was that you had to move all the classroom desks, put up the table at 7.00 and put the lot back as you had found it at 9.00. Can you imagine that being done today? I have no idea who devised this rule but at the end of each game the winner stayed on and the loser made way for the next player in line. This presented a real problem as the rookie players like me sometimes only got to play a couple of times during the whole evening whereas the good players got even better with the many games they played. By playing about three nights each week I slowly got more game time, as well as being an expert desk mover, to the point where I was selected to play in the team where we played in a league against other youth club teams.
   To radically improve our game the team booked two tables for three hours at Platts Billiard Hall in Longton on Saturday afternoon, only when Stoke City were away of course.
   At this point I had the second of my great sporting moments. For those readers who do not play table tennis, the winner of a game has to score 21 points. Picture the scene. We are playing

against Woodhouse youth club in Longton. I am playing in the last game, we are one point ahead and I have to win to ensure that we win the match. My opponent was obviously giving me a hard time as I got to the point where I was losing 20-12. He wanted one point and I wanted nine points so the thought came into my mind 'This would be a good one to win'.

In these circumstances the aim is to just make sure that you get the ball back over the net in the hope that he will eventually make a mistake. Slowly I progressed to the magical 20 marked. If I reached that point then we would have to play on until one of us got two points ahead. As I reached 18 he began to get rattled and you could cut the tension in the crowd of ten with a knife. Suddenly, I reached twenty points and, by this time, I was unstoppable, winning a famous victory for the team. The euphoria was short lived however as due to the late finish and victory celebration, we missed the last bus and had to walk back home!

My career in table tennis carried on when, with a couple of others from the Meir Youth Club team, I joined the Caroline Street team in Longton. To give you some idea of the popularity of table tennis in the 1950s there were about 10 or 11 leagues in the local area with each league having about 12 teams and a promotion and relegation system. We were a midtable in the fifth league team so, for me that was OK. Eventually two of the team moved on to play in the top division and to represent Staffordshire whereas I carried in my usual enthusiastic but mediocre manner. As well as continuing to play table tennis I also found that symbol of a misspent youth…

11. SNOOKER

I think at Platts Billiard Hall in Longton there were about 13 tables on two floors with four table tennis tables on the third floor. Now my Dad, who was born in Longton, was a good snooker player having misspent his youth in Platts to the extent that he once played in an exhibition game there with the legendary world champion Fred Davies.

As a player new to the game you started on the second floor tables, gradually being promoted to the better tables on the ground floor as you improved.

With my friend Kenny, you know that star player at football and cricket in the backs, we would go usually one evening each week plus as many afternoons as we could afford in the school holidays. One afternoon we arrived to find a ton of coke to fuel the heating boiler in the basement piled up outside on the pavement. Imagine our delight when Mr Platt offered us a free table for three hours if we shoveled the coke into the basement. Fortunately, he had two shovels!

In 1960 I married my wife Dot and we went to live in Sandon Road. Our next door neighbour Ted who was about 15 years older than us but a great neighbour and his brother Bob were snooker players so Friday night was snooker night, at Platts of course. Bob would pick us up with his motorbike and sidecar and I would travel luxury class in the sidecar. The maximum break in snooker is 147 which involves clearing all the balls in one visit to the table. My best score ever was a break of 36 yet another example of my limited skills but as good as anything that Ted and Bob could produce. After being an underwhelming success at two indoor sports, I thought that there must be something that I could do well so I started…

12. CYCLING

I had my first bike when I was 10, a Hercules heavy, black totally unromantic bike with not even dropped handlebars, unlike today when most kids start riding at 4 on their lightweight, colourful bikes. Obviously with that bike I was never going to be a road racer and I had never heard the word velodrome. The good thing however was that there were many fewer vehicles on the road so bike riding was an essential part of life with bike racks at every factory or in my case for going to cricket practice or train spotting at Stableford or Whitmore.

Now at my Dad's fruit and vegetable shop he always had an errand boy as did the grocers and butchers. You had to be thirteen to be an errand boy and as most boys left school at fifteen a new boy arrived on the scene every two years. When Freddy, his current errand boy reached fifteen I had just passed my thirteenth birthday so I was in line to be the next errand boy. At the same time my pal Kenny became a paperboy at Lewis's paper shop. Not exactly sports, but both jobs that were a great way be outdoors in all weathers, to build stamina and develop a work ethic. Notice I have mentioned errand boys and paper boys rather than errand and paper girls. That would sound strange now, but not then.

Friday night after school and Saturday morning were the errands boys' main hours although the Coop had full time shop boys who doubled as errand boys. As I was about to take over from Freddy, I went with him for a couple of weeks to learn where all the customers lived. As we

were coming down Weston Road on our way back to the shop we were on the bend at the top of Woodville Road with Freddy leading the way when a lorry overtook Freddy clipping his bike as he passed. The bike mounted the pavement crashing into the wooden fence in front of the local Police house. Freddy was launched from his bike, disappearing over the fence and hedge before crumpling in a heap on the front lawn. I rushed in to see if he was ok and he spent the next fifteen minutes recovering from his accident. When we got back to the shop my Dad was irritated that it had taken us so long with the delivery. I explained everything that had happened, before he looked at Freddy and without asking him if he was ok, he asked him if the bike was alright!! As I was at the High School, I was the errand boy for five years as I did not leave school until I was eighteen. I can only remember one occasion when my Dad got his car out to deliver some of the orders as the depth of snow made it impossible to ride the bike. I was never going to be a champion cycle racer but with all the hills and a heavy bike with up to four orders in the carrier frame, it was a great way to get fit. One order I remember was a lady who had forty pounds of potatoes, two turnips, four pounds of carrots and four pounds of parsnips every week. She could not afford green vegetables and fruit as she had a family of six to feed. On Tuesdays she would walk to the shop for another twenty pounds of potatoes and more carrots and parsnips. A few years after leaving school it was time to play that irritating, exasperating game…

13. GOLF - PART 1

  Now they say that golf is a good way to spoil an enjoyable walk. I was not deterred however and joined two friends Ralph and John who were also starting their golf adventure.
I bought half a set of clubs, a golf bag and some golf balls of course. We joined Leek Golf Club, I had three lessons and we played every Saturday morning at 7.30am, keeping out of the way of the good golfers, to hack our way around the course aiming someday to break the 100 shots barrier. As well as attempting to hit this infuriating little golf ball, or I should say golf balls as we frequently lost them, I had to learn a 'new' language such as Tee, Par, Birdie, Bogey, Eagle and Albatross.
  Now par is the regulation number of shots you should take for each hole 3,4 or 5 shots depending on the distance between the tee and the hole with the flag sticking out of it. At Leek par for the course was 71 shots and, as it was taking us about 110 shots plus you can see that once again my sporting talent, or lack of it, was shining through. You will be asking why anyone would want to put themselves through this torture every week especially in the rain, wind and frost of our winters. Well, the answer is that amongst all this mediocrity every week was the very occasional great shot. This convinced me, or should I say kidded me, that I could at last find a sport that I could be good at. In the event I played the infuriating game for over 30 years mostly with a handicap of 21 or 22. During that time, my friend Brian suggested that we should try…

14. SQUASH

   Now I said that my friend Brian suggested that we should play Squash. I am not absolutely certain about that but whoever suggested it to who, it was a bad idea. Nevertheless, I added a squash racket and some of those small hard rubber balls that generally had a mind of their own, especially when we were hitting them, to my ever-growing collection of sporting equipment.
   We played at the YMCA in Hanley. We had to book a court a week in advance and we could play at any time as long as it was between 10.20 to 11.00pm on a Tuesday evening. So after a day's work and at a time when most sensible people were looking forward to a nights' sleep we were off to play squash. Now a squash court is four walls with a door in one of them to get into the court. Once inside you have to shut the door of course, which was just as well as no one could see what we were up to inside. The reality was that we spent 40 minutes chasing that pesky little ball as it came off at all angles from the walls until we left the court looking like melted butter. After toiling away for months we saw on TV two world class squash players playing the game. Somehow they played the game whipping the ball around the court at a speed that we could only dream of whilst they themselves strolled around the court as their brains calculated exactly where the ball would be at any given moment. Once again reality dawned and Brian returned to his motorbikes whilst I stored away my racket and balls to continue my battle with the golf clubs…

15. GOLF - PART 2

Now it was at this point (1981) that Susan came into my life. She was a 21-year-old American student at Keele University on a 12-month Rotary Scholarship. I was her Counsellor. At Christmas she bought me a book called *Pieces of My Mind* by Andrew Rooney. He wrote an article each week for the New York Times and this book was a collection of his work. One article attracted my attention and was to change my life, for the better of course, otherwise I would not be passing on my secret to you.

It was called 'The Power of Negative Thinking' and it went something like this…

Experts tell us that we dream several times each night. We very quickly forget most of them, but most of us have dreamt of being a sports star, winning a cup or being a world champion. We have all admired and marveled at someone's skill and talent and wondered why it appears far beyond our reach. Why cannot we play football like Xherdan Shaqiri or golf like Rory McIlroy. Most of us have trouble even spelling Xherdan Shaqiri.

Worse still, if it is not Xherdan or Rory, there are a hundred others beyond our reach - our sense of frustration is complete. Wherever we turn, at work, at school or even just cooking at home we see someone whose ability seems to be on a different level to our own. We get so upset

with our own inadequacies that we forget that the people we are trying to emulate have dedicated their lives to being the best. The destructive effect on our life and confidence can be devastating.
　So what is this secret that will lift this cloud from your life?

The answer is simple - Think Negative.

　Hopefully you are reading this book and so, of course can millions of others, but equally many millions of others are illiterate. Get it - forget the relatively small percentage who are cleverer, quicker and more talented than you, instead think about the much larger percentage who cannot do what you do, or at best, are much worse than you. You may have been first reserve in the school football team or bat at number 10 in the cricket team but if there are 60 kids in your school year who don't even make it to number 12 at football and number 10 at cricket, then you have actually achieved something.
　Personally I do not see myself as a Charles Dickens or even a David Walliams, but have you got into print yet?
　We are always being told to think positively, aim high and be the best. How much more comfortable it is to think negative. Be happy with doing the best you can and, if you cannot live with thinking negative, how about thinking positively only of those worse than yourself.

Armed with this advice I was able to approach my sporting ambitions in a completely new way. I didn't have to be good at anything, I just had to participate and enjoy it.

I continued my 'career' in golf but before I tell you more about that, it was at this time that I became…

16. A FOOTBALL MANAGER

My son Gareth could not wait for his ninth birthday as that was the age he could join a Lads and Dads football team. He had been playing boys rugby for two years at Trentham Rugby Club as they could take boys at seven. He enjoyed his rugby but always intended to move on to football when he was nine. The good news for us is that our lawn would get some respite and enable the bare patches to recover even though we constantly moved the position of the goal posts. There was already a Lads and Dads team in Blythe - Blythe Tigers - and they were looking for four new players to add to their squad. On the night twenty boys turned up so about 16 boys were left disappointed, including Gareth. The squad size for a Lads and Dads team was 14.

Harry, the dad of one of the other boys suggested that we could form another team so Blythe Spartans was born with Harry and myself as co-managers. As we were in Leek Moorlands Council area we joined the Leek Moorlands league with teams from Cellarhead, Cheddleton, Leek and Blackshaw Moor. The teams were organised by age with 9s to 11s in the Junior league, 11 to 13 in the intermediate league and 13 to 15 in the Senior league. Harry got a local snooker company to sponsor a strip, we booked a pitch at Blythe High School and we were on our way. What tended to happen was that in the first year you struggled against the boys who were a year older but in the second year we won both the league and the cup with Gareth and winger Andy

It's great that the snooker company are our sponsors. But they've sent 15 red shirts, a black shirt, a pink shirt, a blue shirt, a...
FOOTBALL TEAM SHIRTS

scoring 35 goals between them. It was already pretty obvious that Gareth was a much better player than his dad. The cup final was played at Leek Town's ground and was an exciting experience for the team especially as they won. At the end of each season the League had a presentation evening with the cups and medals presented to the winners. I think that Carl Saunders, then a Stoke City player presented the trophies that year. When we were in the intermediate league, we again reached the cup final at Leek Town ground.

  Unfortunately, we had booked a holiday in Dorset so Gareth was facing the disappointment of missing the Final and, up to that point he had not missed a single game. No problem, we drove down to our holiday home on Friday, left my wife and daughter there on Saturday whilst we drove back home on Saturday night. We played the final on Sunday morning before returning to Dorset to resume our holiday on Sunday afternoon. We lost! After six years in the Staffs Moorlands league Harry finished as co-manager and I took the team into the under 16s league in the Potteries. In my book that was our most successful season. Every week my final instructions to the team was do not use bad language and always accept the referee's decision even if he is wrong. The other plus was that we had a great bunch of dads who had supported the team for seven years and who always accepted that the boys should enjoy their football whatever the result. We finished that season in mid table and at the awards night we won the cup as the league's most sporting team. With a group of 16-year-old boys who, at that point in their lives thought that they knew it all, that beat all the other cups we had won.

Monday the 6th February 1978 was probably one of the worst days in the history of Stoke City. That was the night that they played at home in the FA cup against a non-league team from the North East - Blyth Spartans - the team that we had named our team after. Stoke were having a poor season but should have easily beaten a team full of part time players who the day before and the day after the game were joiners, electricians and office workers etc. The result of the match was Stoke City 2 Blyth Spartans 3. We also discovered that they played in the same green and white colours as us. A couple of years later Gareth was doing a project at school on Hadrian's Wall so we decided to spend a weekend in the North East so that he could see the history of the Roman wall for himself. As we were near Blyth we decided to see if Blyth Spartans had a home game on the Saturday. When we arrived at the ground it was deserted as Blyth were playing away but as we stopped outside a man approached us to see if he could help. By good fortune he was the club Chairman. We explained why we were there and he immediately took us into the club trophy room. It was full of the memorabilia of that night in Stoke. What was a disaster for Stoke City was the greatest night in the history of Blyth Spartans, one of the biggest upsets in the history of the FA Cup.

When Stan Matthews was celebrating his 70th birthday at the Kings Hall in Stoke, one boy from each of the local Lads and Dads league was chosen to form a guard of honour. Gareth was fortunate enough to be the boy chosen from the Leek Moorlands league. A great occasion for him although when I saw the photograph of him with Stan it was obvious that the photographer had not asked Gareth to say cheese.

As an offer to manage Manchester United did not materialise I continued my quest to play something to at least an acceptable level…

17. GOLF - PART 3

When you feel that you can consistently hit that little white ball and, more importantly, keep it on the fairway for at least most of the time, it is time to get a handicap. At that time, to get a handicap you had to compete in the club monthly medal competitions and then record your score countersigned by your playing partner to ensure that you did not cheat. On this particular day I handed in my card to the club professional Peter who said that I had qualified to enter into a national competition organised by Stylo golf shoes to which I answered, what competition? He explained that to qualify you had to score a birdie on the thirteenth hole of your own course. Now the thirteenth hole at Leek is a par three so, on that day, I had played from the tee to sinking the ball into the hole in two shots. I can tell you that in the nearly 20 years of playing at Leek I rarely hit the green with my tee shot, only ever sunk the ball in three shots on about four or five occasions and only once sunk the ball in the hole in two shots. That was the day. Out of something like 600 members only three of us got an entry form. The second part of the competition was bizarre. I had to complete the form by writing a limerick! The winner of the competition got a week's golf in Spain, there were three sets of golf clubs up for grabs and some pairs of Stylo shoes. At this point I had a prize winning thought. My secretary at work had two teenage boys so I asked her if they would write some limericks for me. They sent me three, one of which I thought was really good, so I completed my form and submitted it. To my amazement

I won a full set of Stylo golf clubs so I was able to pass on my half set to my cousin as he had decided to spoil a good walk by taking up the sport. A presentation evening and buffet was organised and the Chairman of Stylo came down from Yorkshire to present me with the clubs, I suppose that you could say that amongst the years of sporting abject failure this was my 10 minutes of fame but not without the help of those two teenage boys. I do hope no one at Leek Golf Club or Stylo reads this book as I might have to pay for the buffet or return the clubs or, even worse, be accused of fraud.

  I was now the proud owner of a new set of clubs, a free buffet and a handicap. In my case it was 22. That means that I could play against Jack Nicklaus take 21 more shots than him and if he only played to his handicap of 0, I would beat him. Dream on and instead apply the Power of Negative Thinking, you know it makes sense. The only reason that you carry on for years and years playing this frustrating game is that almost every week you hit a good shot and just sometimes, a great shot. One such moment was the over two hundred yards par 3 eleventh hole at Leek. The first good thing I did was to hit the ball straight from the tee instead of the usual slice into the trees and long grass. The ball bounced just in front of the green, rolling slowly across the green before disappearing into the hole. I had achieved every golfers dream shot - a hole-in-one. The only downside is that you were expected to leave money on the bar to buy members a free whisky! Years later I achieved the impossible once again when I shot another hole-in-one at Uttoxeter with the inevitable subsequent help for the Scots whisky industry. For the record in nearly thirty years of playing golf I never got my handicap below 21 and the best score I ever achieved was a net round of 85.

  My years of frustration and inconsistency with the game were finally ended when my long time partner Graham became ill and for over a year I did not play. Thankfully Graham made a complete recovery and continues to enjoy his golf but I resisted the temptation to start playing again. As I said earlier golf spoils a good walk but fortunately we had always, with our friends enjoyed…

18. WALKING

   Saturday was walking day and as our friends Pat and Vi lived near Whitmore and we lived in Blythe Bridge, one week we would go East to Leek and the Peak District and the other week West to Shropshire or of course stay in Staffordshire. Amongst our various walking books, we had Les Lumsden's book of pub walks in the Peak District. I think that we have done most of them usually starting and finishing at a pub car park. That was the most important part of any walk in that there had to be a pub either as part of the walk or very nearby.

   Usually we did the walk before going into the pub for a sandwich or hot lunch and a drink, which was fine, but occasionally there would be another pub half way through the walk. Now, it is fatal to stop at that pub no matter how inviting it looks especially if it had an open fire on a cold winter's day. Inevitably we would get too comfortable and eat too much lunch to be then faced with another three to four mile walk back to our car with the added guilt that the car had been parked on the first pub car park without them having the benefit of our custom. The other problem we occasionally had was with Les Lumsden's directions. 'Cross the field to a stile in the bottom right hand corner of the field'. Fine, except that we would trudge to the bottom right hand corner of the field to find no stile and no way out of the field. Ok, by now our book was nearly 10 years old so the paths could have changed, or we might have taken a wrong turn earlier in the walk but when confusion reigned Les Lumsden was certainly not our friend as once you had gone wrong it was very difficult to know where and when the mistake had occurred and as I was usually the keeper of the book to read out the instructions to the rest of them, it was always my fault. I never quite understood why nobody else volunteered to have the book! Another good reason to fall back on The Power of Negative Thinking. Overall and despite the weather on many occasions, we had many enjoyable if sometimes strenuous walks. Now we have got to the stage where the walks have to be shorter and flat with no stiles and muddy fields, so the canal-side paths are now our popular choice. Having decided that golf was too frustrating and inconsistent and country walking becoming more difficult it was time for me to join a…

19. GYM

   Inevitably, when I stopped playing golf I put weight on as that seven stone wet-through teenager who you could hardly see if I stood sideways had evolved into a 15 stone man with a paunch. I had developed the paunch some years earlier and I had failed to convince people that really I had a hollow back. But when my granddaughter said one day "Are you having a baby grandpa?" I thought that I had to do something about it. I signed up for the Nuffield gym just by the bet365 Stadium, the home of the Mighty Potters (more of that later). A fitness trainer gave me a training plan, 10 minutes on the treadmill, 10 minutes rowing and 10 minutes cycling. Initially, 10 minutes on the treadmill was fine, but five minutes on the rowing machine and I was done, with hardly anything left for the cycling. In addition, I did a couple of machines in the weights room.

   My routine, that I have kept to unless I have had a winter cold, is to leave home at 7.00am to beat the rush hour traffic on the A50 on three mornings each week. I gradually built up the amount of exercise I did to the point where I now do at least two miles walking, four to six miles on the cycle and up to 2000m on the rowing machine with the added bonus that my weight dropped from almost 15 stone to just over 14 stone. I can hear some readers saying 'boring' or 'a gym is not for me'.

As a teenager I learned to play the clarinet and later the saxophone and I found that the discipline of a weekly lesson helped me to progress so the routine of a regular visit to the gym works for me. Once there, I can watch the television with my headphones on and, more importantly, as I go on the same days and at the same time each week I meet and have made new acquaintances where we solve the problems of the world and very often discuss the hopes and dreams of our local football teams…

20. STOKE CITY and PORT VALE

Saturday 5th October 1946. My dad took me to my first Stoke game on this date, when Stoke beat Sheffield United 3-0 with the legendary Freddie 'Nobby' Steele scoring all three goals in front of a crowd of nearly 30,000. I don't think that the great Stan Matthews played that day as he was in dispute with the club and was on the brink of being transferred to Blackpool. I only saw one other game that season in March 1947 when Stoke drew 1-1 with Portsmouth thanks again to another Freddie Steele goal.

  After Stan's move to Blackpool, the first time that he played back at the Victoria Ground was on the 27th December 1947 when the gates were locked with over 45,000 inside. I was just 10 years old at the time and my Dad took me to the game. When we got to the Victoria ground the stadium was already full to capacity and the gates were locked with hundreds outside. As Dad was only a short man we usually took with us into the ground a small fruit box to stand on, can you believe that. We always went into the Butler Street Paddock. The box was for me so I always carried it but when we got into the ground dad stood on the box to get a better view whilst I sat on the sloping wall at the side of the paddock entrances or on the pitch side wall. The game started but rather than go home we stood by one of the locked turnstile doors, banging on the door about every 10 minutes in the hope that a steward inside would take pity on us and let us in. About 10 minutes before half time I pushed at the door and to everyone's amazement it opened. I dived under the turnstile, my Dad jumped over followed by 10 or 20 others. Some ran into the paddock whilst we ran up the stairs into the Butler Street stand. As there were no empty seats the stewards easily spotted us and about 6 others sitting on the wooden steps in the gangway. To our amazement, instead of throwing us out they allowed us to stay for the rest of the game. If my memory is correct I think that the game ended a 1-1 but who cared, we had seen the great Stanley Matthews. Those were the days. We did not even need the fruit box that day!

By the following season I was going to most home games on the bus with my friend Kenny and we were Boothen enders. Being children, if you wanted to see the game you either had be at the front behind the pitchside wall or, if you were very thin you could squeeze between the steel framing and the corrugated sheeting at the back from where we watched many games. My next recollection however was the game against Manchester United on the 16th October 1948. As now Man Utd were a top team and when we got to the stadium the Boothen End was full forcing us to go to the Stoke End, we found ourselves about a third of the way up the terracing surrounded by men much taller than us all crammed together so that we could hardly breath. As we stood there waiting for kick off a message came over the tannoy asking some in the Stoke End terracing to move closer together as there were thousands waiting to get in! It was at that point that we thought that it would be a good idea to be…

21. PROGRAMME SELLERS

We got 3 dozen programmes each and our patch was the Boothen End corner of the Butler Street stand, which was good as that was where supporters came to the turnstiles from the car park - at that time only a quite small car park was needed for a 40,000 crowd. We got a farthing for every programme we sold at 3d each so by kick off we had earned nine pence in old money. There was a wide passage between the Butler Street stand and the Boothen End so at just after kick off we would walk down the passage then along the cinder track surrounding the pitch before delivering our takings into the office in the Boothen stand, then emerging back onto the track to walk down to our regular spot in the Boothen End, all this while the game was in progress. Ok we missed the first 15 minutes of the game, but we had money in our pockets to buy fish and chips and the bus fare home and we had seen the game for nothing. After a while we gave up selling programmes so that we could concentrate or our new passion as…

22. AUTOGRAPH HUNTERS

At this time, I had moved from junior school to Longton High School and in my class was Sammy, a boy who lived in Lonsdale Street in Stoke which was near the Victoria Ground. Unlike nowadays, all matches except for Bank Holiday Mondays and Cup replays were played on Saturday afternoon so on Friday I had a briefing from Sammy about the visiting team. He knew whether the team would be coming by coach or train and whether they might be having lunch at the North Stafford Hotel. The favourite football magazine was Charles Buchan's Football Monthly which was full of articles and, more importantly, pictures of the teams and players. I had a hard backed exercise book with two or three pages for each team with pictures from the magazines pasted into the book. On Friday night I would mark the appropriate pages with elastic bands and paper clips so that I could open the book quickly at the right page to get the player to sign over the picture. Now obviously we had to get to the ground or Stoke Station early as the players would arrive an hour or so before the game if they were going to the ground or earlier if they came on the train or going to the North Stafford Hotel for lunch. When Stan Matthews was transferred to Blackpool the number 7 shirt was taken by George Mountford and then by Johnny Malkin. To get the Stoke we would walk down Woodville Road to catch the bus at Meir Square. Now Johnny Malkin lived in a council house in Woodville Road so he would ride on the same bus as us and many other supporters before walking down Lonsdale Street to the ground to play in front of 40,000 supporters. It seems unbelievable in this modern age of millionaire footballers but in those days that was quite normal.

In the early 1950s Stoke were at home to Spurs in a Monday Bank Holiday game. Sammy had informed us the they were coming from London on the train with a bus meeting them outside the Station to take them to the ground. At noon the train arrived and the players walked out of the station and onto the bus. This was the time of the famous 'push and run' team managed by Arthur Rowe and with such legendary players as Ted Ditchburn, Bill Nicholson and Alf Ramsey who would later win the World cup as England manager. There were about 20 of us who were keen autograph hunters but that day I was first on the bus going down both sides of the bus getting every player's autograph. Again something that would be impossible today and, incidentally, you could read every name unlike the unintelligible scrawl used by players today.

On another occasion Stoke played Wolves and at the end of the game Billy Wright who was then the England Captain emerged with his girlfriend, later his wife, Babs of the famous singing group the Beverley Sisters. They were walking to the station to catch a train so about 10 of us walked with them pestering and pleading with him for his autograph. He flatly refused to sign anyone's book and, as we got to Glebe Street bridge I was the only one still following them so he finally stopped to sign his name in my book. A great result but Billy Wright was never quite my favourite player after that.

As autograph hunters we naturally had to go to Port Vale matches so every Saturday was football Saturday. My informant Sammy told us that the Exeter City team playing at Vale Park would be having their lunch at the North Staffs Hotel, so with the team bus parked outside Kenny and I waited for the players to finish their pudding so that we could get their autographs. When all the players were on the bus the driver asked us if we were going to the game. Now the Vale had only just moved from the Old Recreation Ground in Hanley to their new stadium in Burslem and as the driver did not have the benefits of a street map or Sat Nav we had a free ride to the game as we directed the driver to Vale Park. Can you possibly imagine that happening today?

One of my prized autographs was Bert Williams, the Wolves and England goalkeeper and a real gentleman. He had his own Annual, the Bert Williams Football Annual so when Wolves came to town, in addition to my normal autograph book, I also took my Annual. I got his autograph which he signed in the Annual but sadly some years later I lost the book.

Sammy also told me that if you sent a team photograph to the legendary Billy Liddell who was a Scottish international and Liverpool player he would return it, so I sent a team photo which came back a few days later signed by all the players which included Bob Paisley as he was a Liverpool player at the time.

Now, when I look through my old autograph book I realise that there are many internationals all of whom played for either England, Scotland Wales or Ireland. There were few, if any, foreign players in my book. Some interesting autographs included Derek Dooley a centre forward for

Sheffield Wednesday whose career was ended when he had a leg amputated following a football injury, Don Revie who played for Manchester City and who later became the England manager and, of course the great Stan Matthews.

  Two other things stand out, firstly that many players played for the same club throughout their careers and secondly you could almost always read the player's signature. Having mentioned them earlier I have to at least talk about…

23. PORT VALE

I went to my first Port Vale game when they played at the Old Recreation ground in Hanley, now the site of the Hanley Shopping Centre and I remember watching two or three games there before they moved to Burslem in 1950. Naturally, as autograph hunters, Kenny and I were also Port Vale supporters during the memorable 1953/54 season. In that season with the Stoke City legend Freddie Steele as their manager, Vale won the Third Division North League championship conceding only 21 league goals (a record) in the 46-game season and only five goals at home. We missed only one home game that season.

Very few boys who lived in Meir supported Port Vale, as the other end of the Potteries for many adults, never mind young boys, was a foreign country. We went on the train from Meir station to Stoke and then on the famous Knotty, stopping at Hanley and Cobridge, before arriving in Burslem. A quick walk through Burslem Park took us to Hamil Road and the stadium which at that time had a 48,000 capacity. After the game and having waited for the players to leave the ground, we walked down Hamil Road to one of the two fish and chip shops in Waterloo Road, I think that they were about 4 doors apart before catching the train back to Meir. Now many of the carriages on the train were just compartments with no corridors. As we usually had a compartment to ourselves one of our favourite tricks, as the train was pulling out of Normacot station, was to climb on the seats to remove the light bulbs so that we could go through Meir

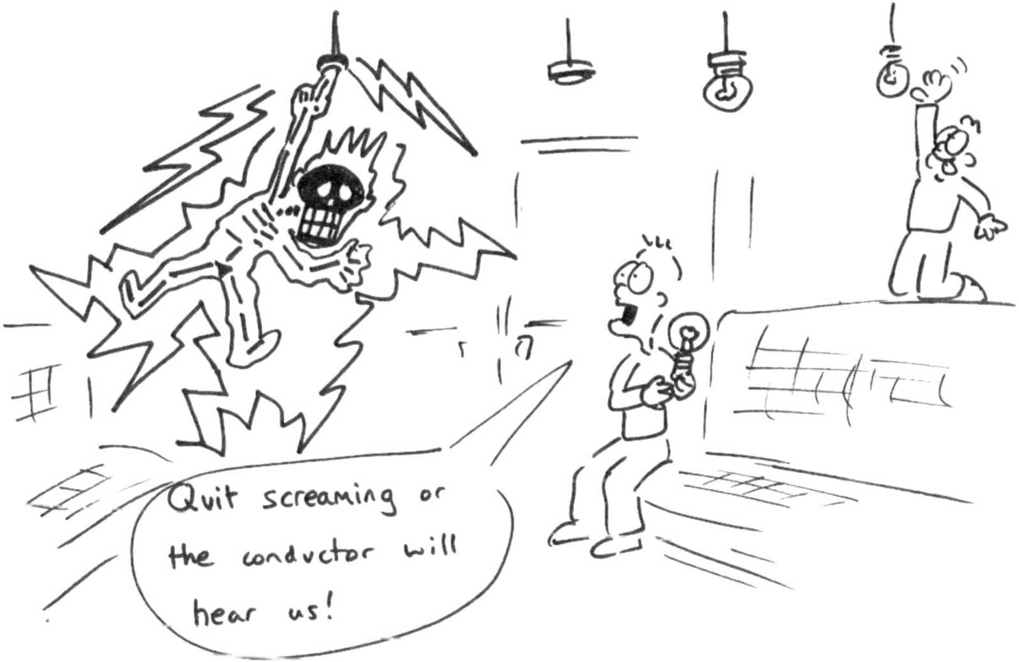
Quit screaming or the conductor will hear us!

tunnel in pitch darkness before quickly replacing the bulbs before we arrived at Meir Station. We never damaged a seat or broke a bulb - honest Officer!

It was also the season that the Vale reached the semi-final of the FA cup. We went to the second-round game at Southport where we drew 1-1 but it was the fifth-round game which caused the excitement, we were drawn at home to the FA Cup holders Blackpool and, of course, the great Stan Matthews. Up to that point in the Cup run, in every round the Vale had been drawn away and in that epic cup run, apart from the second-round replay against Southport, this was the only home cup game. We were in the queue five hours before the turnstiles opened to buy our tickets and after I remember that the queue, four or five deep, zig-zagged across the car park before going to the top of Hamil Road where it meets High Lane.

On the day we were by the wall to the left of the goal at the Hamil end. Fortunately, the Vale left back Stan Potts kept Stan quiet for most of the game resulting in an amazing 2-0 win. After another away win at Leyton Orient we were in the Semi Final of the FA Cup, only the second Third Division team ever to reach an FA cup Semi Final. We were drawn against West Bromwich Albion at Villa Park.

After another day of queuing at Vale Park, we had our two tickets for the open end of the ground at Villa Park. We were still in the days when many people did not have a car so on the day 16 trains steamed from Stoke to Birmingham. The gates opened two hours before the kick off and we were in the ground to get our best vantage point when the gates opened. I remember that we were about half way down the terracing in front a metal crush barrier. I cannot remember much about the game except that every time the ball came quickly down to our end, the crowd behind us swayed down the steps like a wave with us jamming our hands on to the metal barrier to save us from being crushed. It seemed like half the over 68,000 crowd was bearing down on us. We were drawing 1-1 with only a few minutes to go when Stan Turner gave away a penalty and our dream of Wembley was extinguished. Some old black and white newsreel film later showed that it was not a penalty as the foul tackle was outside the area so yet again one of our local club's dream was frustrated by a bad refereeing decision. West Brom went on to play Preston in the Final which they won 3-2. I was convinced that if we had beaten West Brom in the semi-final, the Vale would have gone on to do the impossible - win the FA Cup.

 Another magical Port Vale moment was the 25th January 1964 when Third Division Port Vale were drawn away at First Division Liverpool at Anfield in the 4th round of the Cup. The atmosphere with the Kop in full voice was amazing but even more amazing was the result, 0-0 to set up a reply on the Monday night at Vale Park. Three things I remember clearly about that game, firstly the Kop singing the Beatles songs. Secondly with about 10 minutes to go in the game the ball came in from the right wing across the Liverpool goal and the great Jackie Mudie, a Vale player at the time, slid in to miss the ball by inches to set up what would have been one of the greatest giant killing exploits in Cup history and thirdly at the end of the game the Vale centre half John Nicholson who was a Liverpool boy ran to the Kop with his arms in the air. As you would expect from the Kop crowd they gave him a great ovation. John was later transferred to Doncaster Rovers where he sadly died in a car accident. The replay was played two days later at Vale Park. The official crowd that night was officially just over 42,000 but estimates put the crowd at about 50,000 as thousands broke through one of the gates. We were crammed into the Bycars end and I remember fans climbing up the floodlight pylons and any other roof or vantage point. This time the game went to extra time before Liverpool won 2-1.

Years later, I had my business in Wolstanton and for about five years we sponsored local club Wolstanton United. As a sponsor I was invited as a guest to their Christmas Party. The honorary club President was Jackie Mudie and we usually sat together on the top table. He told me a wonderful story about that Liverpool game. I reminded him that he almost scored a sensational winner and he confirmed that he was desperately close to reaching the ball. He did not play in the replay as he was injured but Freddie Steele was determined that the legendary Liverpool manager Bill Shankly did not find out that Jackie was injured. At that time, you did not have to name your team an hour before kick-off so when Jackie arrived at the ground in his suit and overcoat, Freddie ordered him to stand in the shower area until kick off. Jackie recalled that about every 10 minutes in the hour before the game there was a knock on the dressing room door. Freddie opened the door to be confronted by a barking Bill Shankly asking "Is he playing". Freddie closed the door without answering until 10 minutes before kick off when he finally

admitted that Jackie was not playing and Jackie could at last escape from the showers. Inevitably, when my autograph hunting days finished once I started to work, there was only one club for me…

24. STOKE CITY

Following the Blyth Spartans fiasco, another memorable disaster was on 31st January 1953, again in the FA cup when we played away at Halifax Town who, at that time, were playing in the Third Division North to crowds of a few thousand. With thousands of Stoke fans Kenny and I steamed up to Halifax confident of an easy victory. That day nearly 35,000 packed into the Shay Stadium. They should have called it the shale stadium as most of us were on ash slopes with a few crush barriers thrown in to stop us all finishing in a heap on the pitch. We lost 1-0 and at the end of the game I was convinced that all 35,000 of us left the ground through one pair of gates. The crush was frightening and looking back to those times, it is amazing that there not many crowd disasters. To complete a miserable season for the Potters we were relegated to the second division where we would spend the next 10 years.

In 1963 the Potters were back in the First Division with the start of the great Waddington years after he had taken over as Manager in 1960. My main memory of that season was the away match at Manchester Utd. Just after half time we were losing 2-1 but we were all over United with every hope that we could win the game. Although one of my all-time greats Dennis Law had scored one goal, he had been man marked out of the game by Eric Skeels. As Stoke threw the kitchen sink at United, in the space of about 15 minutes Dennis scored another three brilliant goals to win the game 5-2. What a player.

Now, everyone will have an opinion of who was the best of the Waddington years players. For me apart from the obvious ones who most supporters would agree on like Stan Matthews and Gordon Banks, for me the great players were Dennis Viollet, who was signed from Manchester United on the day we beat Leicester City 5-2 in a league match, George Eastham and Jimmy Greenhough. Matt Busby conceded later that Dennis was the best player he ever let go although at least their dressing room would be less polluted by cigarette smoke after he had gone. I know that many fans will say what about Alan Hudson but George with his silky skills and 100% effort throughout the game was the man for me and Jimmy's pace and shooting was a joy.

On the other hand, who would ever forget Eddie Clamp and George Kinnell. Eddie was described as mad by the then Stoke City trainer Frank Mountford. It was said that he would arrive in the dressing room about 15 minutes before the start of the game having just left the Victoria pub opposite the stadium. In one infamous game against Burnley when we lost 4-3, I remember him jumping to head the ball which he missed by about 5 yards before headbutting the Burnley winger John Connelly. In Stan Matthews autobiography he describes being poleaxed by Chelsea's Chopper Harris. Eddie angrily confronted Harris only to be admonished by the referee. His angry reply to the referee was "That's the trouble with you referees. You don't care who wins the game". Stan recalled that as one of the greatest lines ever said on a football pitch.

My favorite tough tackling George Kinnell memory was against Blackpool who had a young talented Alan Ball in their side. Bally must have upset George as he ran after him with the probable intention of killing him. Fortunately, Alan could run faster as he ran to the Boothen End corner flag shouting for the referee to come and save him.

In the late 1980s Alan Ball returned to Stoke, firstly as assistant to Mick Mills and then very shortly after as Manager. Unfortunately, he did not bring us much success as we were again relegated, this time to the third division for the first time for 63 years. He may have not been a great manager but he did wonders for shares in flat cap makers as he snatched off and threw his cap on the floor at least three or four times in every game.

My son Gareth was born on the 19th September 1974. On the 18th, Stoke were playing Ajax in the UEFA cup at the Victoria ground. The nurse at the hospital told Dot to be at the hospital at 7.00pm so that they could induce the birth. Sorry I said, she will have to come in at 5.00pm so that I would not miss the kick off. I think that they have both forgiven me.

No memories of the Waddington years would be complete without those two wonderful seasons when we reached the semi-finals of the FA cup.

In the first year we were drawn against Huddersfield Town at home in the fourth round. We drew 3-3 forcing a replay at Huddersfield on Wednesday night the 26th January. Once again thousands of fans made the journey over the Woodhead Pass on a cold, windy and very wet night. With about 10 minutes of extra time to play and with the score still at 0-0, their centre forward received the ball in the centre circle with no defenders between him and Gordon Banks in goal. As he splashed through the mud towards our goal Dennis Smith who was 20 yards from him in the left back area gave chase. It was obvious as he approached the penalty area that Dennis was not going to be able to make a fair tackle. Suddenly Dennis took off Superman style flattening their player just outside the penalty area. The resultant free kick was scrambled away and as there were no penalty shootouts the game went to a second replay which we won 1-0 thanks to Jimmy Greenhoff. I cannot imagine how a cold wet car full of fans would have coped with the journey back to Stoke if we had lost that night.

  In the 6th round (one game from the semi-final) that same season we played Hull City away. With my cousin and two of his boys we drove to Hull full of expectation that we were going to reach the semi-final of the FA cup with just one more game before the magic of a final at Wembley. We were on the open end of the ground and as it was in the days just before the fans were segregated, we stood next to two Hull fans. For an hour before kick-off and for most of the game they entertained us with their banter to the extent that when we found ourselves laughing with tears running down our cheeks and we were losing 2-0! Fortunately, we came back to win the game 3-2 which our Hull fans took with great humour. What a pity that those days will never return.

  This is the point in the story where I have to talk about the team that every Stoke City fan loves to hate…

25. ARSENAL

Arsenal were now the team between us and the FA Cup Final. In the 1980s we were in a taxi in London, when our friendly taxi driver asked me where we came from. Stoke I replied. He then said "If I told you that I was an Arsenal supporter what would you say?". I told him that I would tell him to stop the taxi and let me out immediately. He laughed but still took us to our destination and, like the sucker I am, I still gave him a tip!

The semi-final was at Hillsborough, the home of Sheffield Wednesday and we were packed into the Leppings Lane end. By half time we were already dreaming of the Twin Towers thanks to two goals by John Ritchie. In the second half Arsenal pulled one back but with a few minutes to go we were still in a state of high excitement when Arsenal were awarded a corner, when it was clear to every Stokie that Gordon Banks was fouled. From the corner, the ball came into the penalty box. It was headed by an Arsenal player towards our goal with John Mahoney diving to stop the ball going into the goal with his hand. By this time, we were into the fourth minute of injury time although there had been no injuries or stoppages of any sort. Arsenal scored from the penalty and we all let the stadium in total disbelief. I am sure that every fan from every club in the country, except Arsenal fans of course, thought that Stoke had been robbed. For the record, the referee that day was Pat Partridge, I still have nightmares about him.

The replay was an evening game at Villa Park and as the players were probably as shell shocked as the fans, I think that we all went more in hope than expectation and in front of a crowd of over 62,000 we lost 2-0. There were five of us in my car and we drove up the M6 with thousands of others in complete silence, until just as we were passing the Hilton Park service area one of my friends said "This is the fastest funeral procession I have ever been in".

However, the following season 1971/72 we finally reached a final at Wembley…

26. THE LEAGUE CUP FINAL 1972

Saturday March 16th 1972 is a date etched on every Stoke City supporter's memory, the day that we beat Chelsea to win the club's first major trophy, the League Cup. With over 30,000 City fans, I was there.

I always said that I would never go to Wembley Stadium until Stoke got there. I did get a ticket to the 1956 final and travelled down to London on the train on the day of the final. The real reason for going to London that day was to see Louis Armstrong at Earls Court, so I sold my ticket to a fan at Euston Station.

The problem with the '72 final was that my business partner was getting married that day and I was best man. At least I was until Stoke reached the final. Sometimes you have to get your priorities right!

I managed to get 12 tickets in various parts of the ground for friends and family but as a Boothen Ender I wanted to be behind the goal at the Stoke end of the stadium with the real fans. The day was perfect when TC scored the first goal and George Eastham, my favorite Stoke player at the time, scored the winner. The excitement level was so high after George scored that second goal that I don't remember anything about the game except the infamous back pass by Micky Bernard that was thankfully saved by the best goalkeeper in the world Gordon Banks.

For me however the following day, Sunday, the day the team brought the cup home, turned out to be even more memorable as I was on the coach with the players on that amazing journey from Barlaston Station to Stoke Town Hall.

The only open top bus in North Staffordshire was owned by Lymers Coaches of Tean. The bus was hired to carry the team on the understanding that it was driven by the company's owner Aubrey Lymer.

I knew Aubrey through a mutual interest in cine film making, we were both members of Blythe Bridge Cine Group. He also had been to Wembley and I knew that he was driving the bus but never imagined that I would be part of that epic journey.

At lunchtime on Sunday I got a phone call from Aubrey saying that he had been contacted by the police to say that whatever happened he must keep the bus moving. That frankly had frightened him to death and his desperate voice asked me if I would ride with him in the bus to give him some much needed support. I did not realise that the driver's cab was right across the front of the bus so that I would be able to sit next to him.

As a lifelong Stoke City fan I could not believe my luck. Fortunately, I had my camera and some spare cine film and I could not get to Tean quickly enough to begin our journey. We parked up at Barlaston Station surrounded by thousands of fans to await the arrival of the team on the train from London.

The reaction to the arrival of the train and the emergence of the cup in the hands of Tony Waddington was amazing and this was just the start. It seems laughable now but we had just one police car in front of the bus and I think 2 police motorcyclists. At Meir Heath another of our cine club members Bill Townley was filming the bus as it approached and as we almost came to a stop he joined us in the cab.

The first major point of the journey was the Broadway at Meir and as we came down Sandon Road there seemed no way that we were going to get through the crowds. There were thousands of people seemingly blocking our way but slowly the police car forced a path through the crowds who were up lamp posts, on bus shelters, in the windows of the flats and any other vantage point that they could find.

Unfortunately, the train had arrived 45 minutes late at Barlaston so the light was beginning to fade and, as I had no fast film, I had to stop filming.

We continued our journey through Longton and Fenton to the Town Hall at Stoke through ever more excited crowds. As we pulled into the back entrance of the Town Hall we thought what do we do now, Aubrey's job was done and we were not invited to the party. We had other ideas however. We got off the bus among the players went through the door with them, grabbed our free glass of sherry and we were in.

When the players stood on the Town Hall balcony with the cup in front of thousands of cheering fans we were standing just behind them. My memorable weekend was complete.

We later gave the film that we had shot to the club, and it is now on DVD and YouTube. The Sentinel newspaper estimated that 200,000 people were on the streets of the Potteries that day and I would not disagree with that.

Unfortunately, Aubrey died a few years later in a swimming accident in Singapore but the bus has been lovingly restored and can be seen at many events in the area.

As well as winning the League Cup, we were also on course to reach another FA cup semi-final. To every fans horror we were again drawn against Arsenal. This time the game was at Villa Park and as the team had played nearly 70 games that season in the League, the League Cup, the Texaco Cup and the Anglo-Italian Cup so it was probably a game too far as Stoke struggled to a 1-1 draw.

With the replay 4 days later we again took to the road, this time to Goodison Park which we lost 2-1 in the most bizarre fashion. With the score at 1-1, John Radford received the ball when he was clearly nearly ten yards offside to score the winning goal. The linesman admitted later that he had thought that a programme seller on the track on the other side of the pitch was an Arsenal player! Even 'Roy of the Rovers' in the Rover comic paper would not have got away with that story line. Our hate for Arsenal football club was complete.

For the last almost 10 years we have had the satisfaction - courtesy of Tony Pulis - of irritating Arsene Wenger and Arsenal, at least in the home matches. The sight of 25,000 fans doing The Wenger was priceless.

Forty-five years later that famous bus was back on the road accompanying many of the players from that memorable day as they toured the Potteries this time from the bet365 stadium to the Kings Hall in Stoke for a celebration dinner. I was very pleased to accept an invitation from the players to join them on the open top double decker bus together with the Lord Mayor and various press and TV reporters. I was also able to join them in the press room and got to meet my favourite player from 1972, George Eastham. We have two things in common, we are the same age and we both played football. The difference is that he kept his place in his junior school football team and went on to have a glittering career as professional footballer. He now lives in Cape Town but comes back to Stoke every year as his son lives locally. I asked him if he was still involved in football to which he replied "nearly every day". He still coaches boys in Cape Town helping them to achieve the dreams that he, no doubt, had as a boy. The other difference is that he got to wear that Arsenal shirt as he was transferred from Arsenal to Stoke City but I would never hold that against him.

I think at this point I should return to some of the other sports I had no aptitude for…

27. BOXING

  Now, as I was someone who stood aside when some big ugly rugby player from the scrum came running towards me, I was never going to stand in a canvas ring which is actually square (never understood that) to be knocked senseless by somebody who actually enjoyed doing it. I do remember on one occasion wearing a pair of boxing gloves in the school gym but either I was very skilled at avoiding my opponent's punches or, more likely, he took pity on me and did not want to knock my glasses off.

  My Dad however was a boxing fan but, to my knowledge never indulged in the noble art. He took me on a regular basis as a boy to watch professional boxing at the Victoria Hall, where Tuesday night once a month was boxing night. I saw some great fights with all the blood and guts, and the galvanised bucket, sponge and cold water that revived the boxer at the end of each round. I loved the fights where the crowd would throw nobbins (money) into the ring, which as you know is square. To show their appreciation of a good fight, money rained down from the spectators up in the balcony and gallery. I am sure that would not be allowed today!

  On one special occasion in the early 1950s Randolph Turpin, the then undisputed Middleweight champion of the world, fought an exhibition fight with local boxer Larry Parkes. Larry, who is now in his 80s, was elected to boxing's Hall of Fame a few years ago.

I also went with Dad to the amateur boxing nights at the Victoria Hall with tournaments between the local Police boxing club and the Army, Navy and Airforce boxing clubs. On one occasion, during the interval, the compere asked for silence whilst he gave details of a boxing night in Wolverhampton involving the Police boxing club. He carefully explained the date and time and went on to give details of buses that were being laid on the transport supporters to the event. After talking for about five minutes he finally stopped, when a man sitting in the balcony reduced the audience to laughter by shouting "Yer Wha".

The boxing promoter of the professional nights was a little too ambitious however when he hired the Sun Street speedway stadium to promote three British and Empire championship bouts plus a ~~none~~ boxing special appearance by Lee Savold who had recently beaten the British boxer Bruce Woodcock to win a version of the World Heavyweight championship. He also fought boxing legends Joe Louis and Rocky Marciano during his career. Although about 6,000 fans attended, it was a financial disaster, ending the Victoria Hall promotions until many years later.

In the days before TV one of the great joys was listening on the radio to great fights featuring legends like Bruce Woodcock, Brian London and Freddie Mills. As well as boxing my dad also took me to watch…

28. WATER POLO

   My Dad could swim but I never saw him swim. By the age of 10 my grandchildren had gained all their swimming and lifesaving badges, whereas I had never been in more than six inches of water in the bath at home when I started high school at the age of eleven. As we had a swimming pool we all took our trunks and towels on one day a week for swimming lessons. So for two weeks I went into the pool, remembering to take my glasses off and where I had put them. After the second week I caught a cold which nearly always turned to bronchitis. I could never persuade my mother that a cold was an infection. As far as she was concerned you caught a cold from sitting in a draft or getting wet so from that point on I had a note excusing me from swimming. Later, I worked for 50 years and never had more than two days off through illness and only two weeks in total. So much for my mother's medical knowledge and my opportunity be become an Olympic swimmer.
   In the late 40s and 50s there was a local water polo league as all the Five Towns and Newcastle had public swimming schools. At Longton Baths, Saturday night was water polo night and there was always a good crowd watching the matches. That was until 1948 when subsidence caused a large crack across the baths through which all the water disappeared. As you could not play polo without the water that ended that Saturday night excitement. At that time there was also…

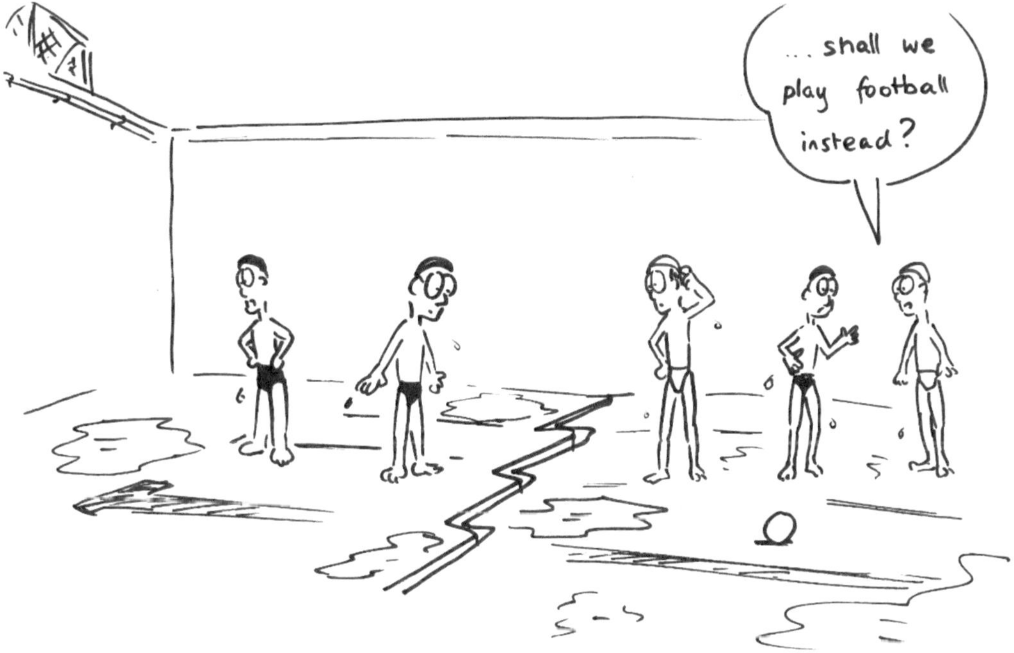
... shall we play football instead?

29. SPEEDWAY

Sun Street stadium in Hanley was the home of Stoke Speedway where iconic names like Ken Adams, Gill Blake, Reg Fearman and a rider – Mitchell - who we called the 'chinless wonder', (chinless probably as a result of a war wound) were our speedway heroes. Racing started after the war at Sun Street in 1947 and in 1949 they were National third division champions. I remember going with my pal Kenny one night that season when the top two teams Stoke Potters and Yarmouth raced in front of a crowd of over 17,000. I was obviously too young to be a star of the speedway world although we spent many hours enjoying cycle speedway at Normacot Rec. Again, there was a local cycle speedway league then, now with many other things, long gone. Another 'sport' if you could call it that to enjoy was…

30. WRESTLING

With my pal Kenny, Saturday night was Wrestling night. In those days the Victoria Hall was almost full every week with wrestling fans eager to see if Count Bartelli and Kendo Nagasaki would be unmasked. They never were, at least not until many years later, as that was one of the reasons the fans returned each week. As well as the fake fights, if a wrestler was thrown out of the ring (which was still square), there was always a couple of elderly ladies on hand to clout them with their umbrellas. Funny how it was always the same ladies sitting in the same ringside seats!

 Kenny and I could not afford ringside seats so we looked down from the cheap seats in the Gallery. It had one great advantage however. We always took some paper with us or bought a programme. Why? I hear you ask. Can you think of a better place to launch a paper airplane during the interval? I strongly advise readers not the try this when they are next in the Victoria Hall as nowadays it is almost certainly in contravention of Health and Safety.

As I said at the beginning of my book *'full of enthusiasm, not much talent'*, but I believe that my love of sport has given me many memorable moments both playing and watching sport. I believe that sport and music are so important in the development of young children and a great way to learn social skills, teamwork and lifetime friends. When we were young, we spent many hours of freedom in the streets and fields with no TV, Xbox or other game machines to tie us to a chair or bedroom. Sadly, that is not possible today so it is even more important that schools and parents give children every opportunity to explore sport and outdoor pursuits.

Finally, you will have noted that the one person that was part of all my childhood sports was my friend…

31. KENNY

Kenny lived with his parents and two brothers in a terraced house at the back of our shop. Unfortunately, the eleven plus exam segregated children between secondary modern school and high school and from that point on our friendship prevailed but our lives went in a different direction. Kenny was just as able as me at school but high school was not an option as his dad considered that it was not the place for him, and this was the case for many others like him. For him the only option was the secondary modern school and work at fifteen. He became Head Boy at Meir Senior school before starting work as an apprentice glazier. It was no surprise to me when one of the partners in the firm told me that he was the best apprentice he had ever employed. As the pressures to earn more money increased he went into the Pottery industry as a polisher. After thirty years and in his early fifties he died with the Potters dust disease.

I would like to dedicate this book to his memory.

ALSO FROM COX BANK PUBLISHING…

Just a Face in the Crowd
By life-long Stoke City supporter Roger Horwood, this is a journey through time, featuring his memories of seeing Stoke's greatest football heroes - including Stanley Matthews, Gordon Banks, and Alan Hudson. With 45 individual stories spanning seven decades.   In support of the Sir Stanley Matthews Coaching Foundation.

SPLASH!
An anthology of swimming poetry and artwork from Hillside Primary School, SPLASH! is designed to be a writing and drawing book too. With work from the whole school, from the Reception class to Year 6, plus local poets. Add your own poems and art! In support of the Royal Life Saving Society.

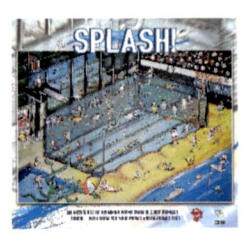

HEROES!

What happens when your school football team is threatened with disaster? An exciting adventure story featuring a host of local sporting heroes, who all help try to get the school team get to the World Schools Football Cup Final. Will they make it? Can they overcome monsters, tornadoes, volcanoes and more? And can they save the world from asteroid impact? Follow superheroes Jess and Jack from Seabridge Primary School as they take on their first mission. In support of the Donna Louise Trust and Seabridge Radio.

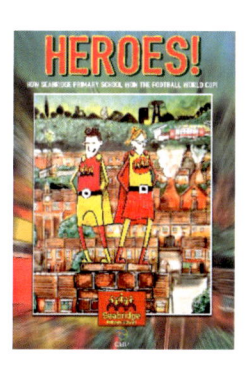

RUN! This School Loves… Running!

RUN! is an anthology of writing and illustration celebrating Stoke-on-Trent's running school – the Willows Primary School in Penkhull. With contributions from across the school, this is a book to read and be inspired by. And then go for a run… A contribution from each book sold will go to the charity Lucas' Legacy, in support of childhood brain cancer research.

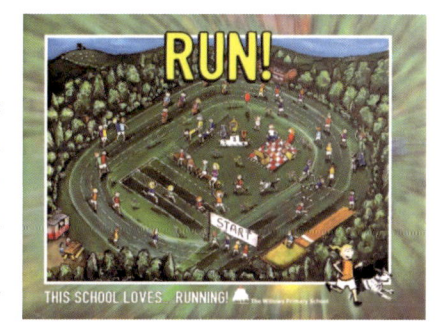

'Arf Marathon

The story of a half marathon, the ever-popular Potters 'Arf, with contributions from over 60 participants. See the race from every perspective: runners, walkers, volunteers, organisers, charities and more. 13.1 miles of blood, sweat, tears and laughter. In support of the Douglas Macmillan Hospice and the Donna Louise Trust.

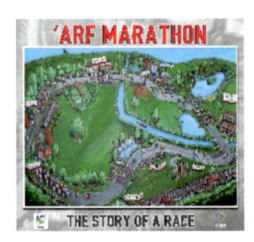

The Cat & Fiddle Cycling Challenge

An anthology of writing by cyclists, *The Cat & Fiddle Cycling Challenge* features personal stories from Brian Rourke Cycles' popular charity event. Starting and finishing in Stoke-on-Trent, this 55-mile ride winds through Staffordshire, Cheshire and Derbyshire and includes the infamous 7-mile Cat & Fiddle climb. Drawn from the 2016 and 2017 events, the stories give a flavour of the highs, lows, laughs and tears this event brings year after year. Proceeds from the book are in support of Cystic Fibrosis Care.

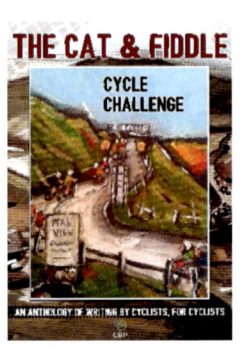

Sporting Stories: Stoke-on-Trent City of Sport 2016
Volume one of the *Active City Stories* series and the first of three books covering the city of Stoke-on-Trent. Over 80 contributors tell their stories of what being active means to them. With more than 30 sports and activities covered, there's inspiration for all, and some great artwork too. In support of the Sir Stanley Matthews Coaching Foundation and their work with disabled children.

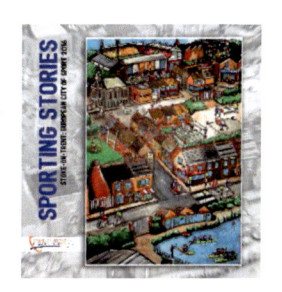

Active City Stories: Stoke-on-Trent
Volume two of the *Active City Stories* series. Yet again, over 80 contributors of all ages from 4-year-olds upwards tell their stories of what being active means to them. The writing – and lots of children's artwork too – was collected in the course of 2017 from runners, football fans, swimmers, trampoliners, rising taekwondo stars, budding artists and more, all writing or drawing about the joy of being active.

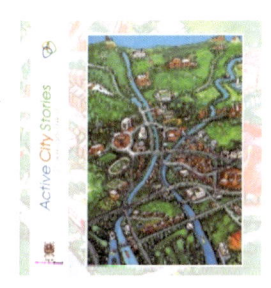

All our books are available online at www.coxbankpublishing.com/shop **, on Amazon or from your local bookshop.**